THE WISDOM OF SMALL THINGS

R. VENKATARAM

BookLeaf Publishing

India | USA | UK

Made with ❤ on the BookLeaf Publishing Platform
www.bookleafpub.in
www.bookleafpub.com

To the Seekers of Truth,

To the Architects of Ideas

&

To the Guardians of Wonder.

May your journey be boundless

and your discoveries be profound.

Acknowledgements

This book is a reflection of the love, wisdom and inspiration I have been fortunate to receive.

To my entire family, thank you for instilling in me the values of curiosity and perseverance and for always encouraging me to dream big.

To my wife, your unwavering support, love and belief in me have been the cornerstone of this journey. You are my greatest companion in both life and thought.

To my daughter, your innocence and joy remind me of the beauty in simplicity and the wonder in everyday moments.

To my friends and colleagues, whose encouragement and conversations have fuelled my creativity and challenged my perspectives. Your support in this journey and shared moments of laughter and insight have been invaluable in bringing this work to life.

To the countless seekers, whose works have shaped my understanding of the world, I owe my gratitude. Your words have been a beacon of light on this path.

And to you, the reader, thank you for embarking on this journey with me. Your openness to these reflections gives this work its true meaning.

This book is a small tribute to the endless pursuit of truth, love and connection.

···　✳　···

Preface

This book is a journey through questions, reflections and the search for meaning in a world full of possibilities. Each poem is an invitation to pause, to wonder and to seek the truths hidden in everyday moments.

Inspired by the wisdom of family, friends, daily life and the great thinkers who have shaped my life, these words are intended to provoke thought and spark connection. This collection is for those who seek, question and dream. May it offer you a moment of insight and peace in your own journey.

... ✳ ...

Table of Contents

SALUTATIONS TO LORD GANESHA

O Ganesha, Son of Mahesha,
The Intelligent One, Super Stable One,
O Lord divine, with wisdom so fine,
Breaker of chains, Reliever of pain.

As Vyasa's scribe, you took the lead,
Breaking your tusk for a noble deed.
Unceasingly, you wrote the Epic lore,
With truth, knowledge and wisdom at its core.

You bested Lord Kartikeya in the race of the sky,
By circling your parents, who stood nearby.
You humbled mighty Ravana, strong and bold,
Outwitting his greed with a tale untold.
You escaped Lord Shani's grip with a smile,
Proving wisdom travels an eternal mile.

With a Gana's head and a human form,
You gained wisdom beyond the norm.
Named Ganapati, leader of Ganas,
Remover of obstacles, Harbinger of success.
All in Thy grace, let us embrace.

··· ✳ ···

SOORASAMHARAM: THE TRIUMPH OF THE VEL

On the sixth day's dawn, with skies painted gold,
The legend of Skanda Shashti, Hymns and Tales retold.
At Tiruchendur's shore, where waves embrace,
Devotees gather in Murugan's grace.

The demon brothers – Tarakasura fierce,

Simhamukha, with roars to pierce,
Soorapadman, whose strength and guile,
Had cast the heavens in shadows vile.

For six days long, the heavens sighed,
As Lord Murugan's army marched with pride,
Lord Murugan stood, with a vision divine,
With eyes like stars, His purpose aligned.

The Vel, Mother's Gift, His symbol of truth,
Forged in the fires of his boundless youth.
In a fierce battle, the earth did shake,
As Soorapadman's power began to break.

With a swift strike, the Vel did soar,
And struck the demon to rise no more.
On Shashti Tithi's blessed day,
Good triumphed, and darkness gave way.

In every heart, His story we sing,
Of Lord Murugan, the eternal King.
O Skanda, O Vel, forever adored,
Guide us, protect us, our divine Lord.

··· ✳ ···

TO DAUGHTER, FROM FATHER

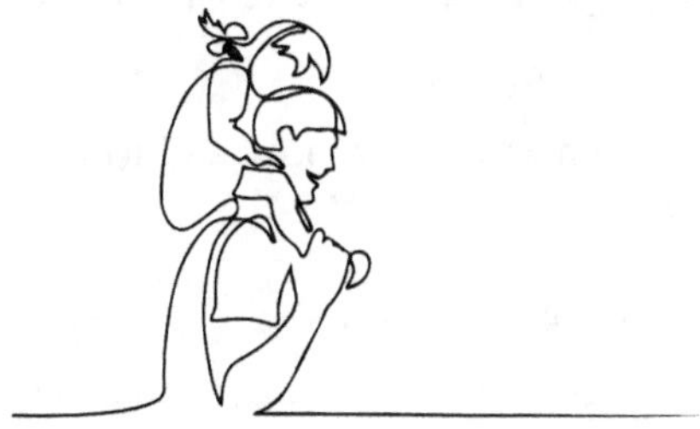

···She requested the poem be placed third because her birthday is on the third!···

My Daughter, the world is big and complex,
It has good people and bad, fairness and
injustice.
You'll face challenges and choices,
And I want to help you navigate them.

I'll teach you to be kind and respectful,
To stand up for what's right,
To think for yourself and trust your instincts,
And to never stop learning.

Before you conquer the world,
You must first conquer yourself.
Understand your fears, control your senses,
know your strengths,
And learn to master your mind and heart.

Life won't always be easy,
But you can rely on your strength and character.
Stay honest, stay humble,
And treat others as you want to be treated.

Remember dear, wherever you go,
My heart walks with you through highs and
lows.
The world is tough, but so are you,
There's nothing dear, you can't do.

You can grow into someone strong and wise,
Someone who makes a difference in this world.
I believe in you, my daughter,
And I always will.

··· ✳ ···

TO MY WIFE

···A poem dedicated to my partner in everything.···

A woman of grace, with a heart so kind.
A soulmate and friend, one of a kind.

A smile that brightens the darkest night.
A love that shines, like a beacon light.

A bond of Trust, A connection True.
A friendship formed between Me and You.

Through laughter and tears, we stand as one.
Together forever, under the sun.

With every step, with every fall.
We lift each other through it all.

A *partner true, a wife, a friend so dear.*
A *treasure to cherish and hold always near.*

IF MY THOUGHTS...

···How does it feel to know your thoughts, words and deeds are in harmony?···

If my thoughts could spark a flame within,

If my thoughts could calm the raging wind,

If my thoughts shaped the dreams you seek,

If my thoughts were for larger well-being,

Then I feel the elation of life.

If my words could soothe your bitter frown,

If my words could help you stand your ground,

If my words made you smile and ponder,

If my words were true & pure reflection of my

THOUGHT,

Then I feel the elation of life.

If my deeds inspired you with beauty,
If my deeds made you still and think twice,
If my deeds showed you a new way out,
If my deeds were true & pure reflection
of my WORDS,
Then I feel the elation of life.

··· ✳ ···

MAHABHARATA

The Mahabharata, a tale of old,
Of Dharma's path, fierce and bold.

Dice rolled, fate sealed in Kuru's hall,
Where cousins clashed and kingdoms fell,
And in each heart, deep stories dwell.

With Krishna's wisdom guiding their way,

Through battle's night and destiny's sway.
Arjuna stood, with a bow in hand,
Torn by the weight of war's demand.
Krishna revealed the cosmic lore,
The Bhagavad Gita, forevermore.

Draupadi's tears, Bhishma's vow
Karna's fate, Vidura's woe,
Dhitharasta's Prejudice, Duryodhana's greed,
Shakuni's deceit, Krishna's wisdom.
Each soul, bound by karma's thread,
Through love, loss and blood, they bled.

A war of justice, of greed, of pride,
Where truth and lies were side by side.
Yet through the darkness, one truth stays:
Dharma lives in mysterious ways.

For in this epic, life's lessons run,
The battle of the self is never done.

Mahabharata teaches, with wisdom and grace,
Life is a war of qualities, each heart must face.

··· ✳ ···

VIDURA: AN EMBODIMENT OF VIRTUE

···Have you ever felt like Vidura – loyal, wise, but standing alone?
How do we maintain integrity in a world full of distractions?···

Within Hastinapura's majestic halls,

Vidura stood, noble as duty calls.

Vidura, Yama Incarnate, steadfast and wise,

A minister of insight, with counsel precise.

Wisdom adorned his every speech,
Dharma's path, he sought to teach.
With righteousness standing by his side,
To justice and truth, his path was tied.

Loyal, yet firm with integrity,
He warned of greed and its futility.
To Dhritarashtra, he earnestly appealed,
'Beware, O King, of Duryodhana's greed'!

Humble in heart, yet strong in deed,
Serving the kingdom, not his own need.
With impartiality, he advised,
Both Pandavas and Kauravas, equal in his eyes.

His foresight saw the coming storm,
The Kurus' fall, in conflict sworn.
For peace he strove, with words so wise,
But war's cruel march could not be denied.

Unaffected by wealth, with detachment pure,
His spiritual strength made his path secure.
Through trials of insults, his patience shone,
A moral compass, who stood alone.

With ethical leadership, he set the bar,
Vidura Neeti, a wisdom-filled guide.
Vidura, the sage, just and fair,
A timeless hero beyond compare.

GANDHI: THE MAN, THE MAHATMA

Gandhi ji, the essence of who he was,

he was a determined seeker of truth,

a humble soul clad in simple khadi,

a fearless voice against oppression,

a torchbearer of peace amidst storms of violence,

an unyielding warrior armed only with
nonviolence,
a tireless weaver of unity in diversity,
a man who turned salt into a symbol of freedom,
a father of a nation, yet a servant of the masses,
an astute strategist, bending empires with
resolve,
a dreamer of a just and equitable world,
a sage who lived his teachings as his testament,

and the undying spirit of ahimsa incarnate.

THE ESSENCE OF PARENTING

Parenting is love that lets children be,

A lighthouse standing by the sea.

Parenting's weight is not to own,

But to guide a soul as they've grown.

To spark their wonder, let curiosity rise,

And lead by example, through loving eyes.

Giving freedom with care, a balance to find,

An atmosphere nurturing heart and mind.

Patience and acceptance, a steady hand,
To guide them gently as they take a stand.
Parents must listen, truly hear their voice,
Spend daily time, making love their choice.
Offer support through every emotion,
Building trust with endless devotion.

A parent knows life's pitfalls deep,
Guiding their child so they don't leap.
If the child willingly shares their joys and strife,
The parent has succeeded in life.

THE MEASURE OF A MAN

···What is the true measure of a man –
his strength or the character he
builds?···

In quiet strength, his virtues shine,
Integrity, the heart of his design.

With kindness woven through his tone,
Compassion breathes in the words he's shown.

He stands for truth, both firm and wise,
In trials faced, his courage lies.

Through storms of doubt, he holds his ground,
A steady will, where strength is found

In laughter shared and burdens borne,
He rises renewed with every dawn.

For in a man's character, we see,
To unwavering truth, come what may.

Perception and intelligence, his guiding force,
Success flows from his vision's steady course.

WOMEN'S SPIRIT

···What lights up her spirit? Courage, love or both?···

In shadows cast where hopes seem thin,
A woman's heart bears the weight within.
With every challenge, she rises anew,
In the face of struggle, her spirit shines through.

In the silence of night, her dreams take flight,
Fighting through battles that dim the light.
With courage unyielding, she charts her own way,
For the strength of a woman will never betray.

In the crowd, she stands, her voice a soft plea,
Navigating paths where few dare to see.
With every scar worn, a story unfolds,
A testament to strength that the heart always
holds.

With every step taken, she shatters the mould.
In a world that confines, her spirit is bold.
Through trials and tears, she learns to arise,
For a woman's true power is found in her eyes.

WILLINGNESS

What can be an Adventure, can also be a
nightmare.
What can be a Sweet Responsibility, can also be
a burden.

What is it? That stands between a love affair and
a rape.
What is it? That stands between volunteering
and coercion.

Same Act, with Diametric Ends!

Willingness, it is, to give into the act, that makes
the difference,
Absolute Willingness is unconditional love,
pure in its essence.
A sweet human emotion, a foundation for
commitment's start,
It births trust, integrity and power within the
heart.

Willingness is spirituality, a guiding light so
true,
It sweetens the passage of life, in all that we
pursue.

INTEGRITY'S LIGHT

···In moments of doubt, does your
integrity lead the way?···

In truthful moments, Integrity takes its stand,
A heart unwavering, a steady hand.
A quiet strength within we find,
Coherence in thoughts, speech and mind.

Adversity tests this virtue true,
Integrity holds, steadfast through.
It needs no rules, no laws to bind,
A faithful compass, within us, we find.

Deception may deceive the eye,
But integrity never tells a lie.
It's doing right, though none may see,
An earnest pledge to honesty.

Integrity nurtures trust to grow,
A fertile ground where success will flow.
Align your words, your heart, your mind,
In this, your truest self you'll find.

Integrity, the leader's creed,
It plants within the finest seed.
It is the foundation that makes us whole,
Integrity – the compass of the soul.

··· ✷ ···

LOVE: THE JOURNEY WITHIN

Love, the sweetest emotion of all,
A boundless gift, possessed by all.
Not something we do, but something we are,
A nurturing force, a blissful spark.

When hearts are open, pure & wide,
Love flows boundless, like the ocean's tide.
A choice, a will, a state of grace,
A firm refuge, a joyful place.

Yet, often we confuse its brief bloom,

When hormones cloud the mind's clear room.
For love is not to possess or bind,
But to expand through inclusion & free the
mind.
For the longing to possess comes from lack,
But true love walks a different track.

A flower it is, tender and bright,
Demanding care, not force nor might.
To extract joy or to demand Love's stay,
Is to risk love to fade away.
A *process of giving, of setting free,*
A *gentle dissolution of 'the me'.*

For love comes with no assured promise,
Its life depends on awareness and nurture, you
see.
When love fills the heart, it shows the way,
Its wisdom guides each day.
A human possibility, vast and true,
Love blossoms within – it begins with you.

… ✳ …

ADULTERY

*···Is the temptation worth the price of
what you stand to lose?···*

A Boundary, crossed by a Lie.
Enough to put all Truths under Shy.

A Love, Not a Love, But a Decoy.
A Mistake, Not a Mistake, But a Choice.

Betrayal, Hurt of the order Highest,
Adultery, Betrayal of the order Deepest,
For in it, Hurt gets compounded Steepest.

Tempting to Give in, an act,
Impossible to Take back, after the enact.

A Violation of Trust,
Relationship's foundation goes Burst.

Cheaters Believe & Live, their own Lie.
Unwilling to listen, even a Pie.

Every Sin comes with a punishment.
And Punishment neither Hurries nor Forgets.

Even if NOT apprehended,
When Adultery Walks In,
Everything Worth Having Walks Out.

··· ✳ ···

SEPARATIONS: WHEN PATHS DIVERGE

⋯Can anything be harder than a divorce?⋯

In life's vast web, relationships are spun,
Each formed to meet a need, a purpose begun.
Physical, Mental, Emotional, a need to cater,
Yet when needs falter, so may the ties alter.

Marriage, they say, is a weaving of two,
A dance of hearts, a merging of views.
Living beyond self, a step so profound,
Daily care keeps love truly bound.

*No bond is absolute; Unless cared, it sways,
Conduct it with grace, through life's winding
ways,*

A spouse is not a stop, but a fellow traveller,
A fellow traveller in this universe.

Sharing joy, not extracting, is the art,
To give all you can, with an open heart.
No tally of gain, no marketplace ploy,
Just a pure exchange of limitless joy.

When every effort, every try has failed,
And no common ground can be unveiled,
Only for larger well-being, Only to save the
peace inside,
Separation may be the path to abide.

Not as a hasty move, nor with disregard,
But as the final choice, when love grows hard.
Not a failure, but a step toward peace,
For sometimes love means letting go to release.

For hearts that are true, love will remain,
Beyond form, beyond loss, beyond any pain.
To part with respect is to honour the past,
For love that was shared, forever will last.

··· ✷ ···

TRUTH AND LIE

···*When was the last time you chose truth over lie? How did it feel?*···

Truth is not just moral or wise,

It's the light where clarity lies.

It builds trust, a cornerstone for unity,

A path to meaningful connection and success.

Being true, owning mistakes, may sting,

But respect and trust it brings.

Lies disrupt, creating doubt and mistrust,

Turning harmony into disarray.

With a single lie, trust will fall,
Truths once strong, now questioned by all.
A mirage of lies may seem so near,
But fades away, leaving only fear.

Truth and Lie, Not only verbal,
Also thrive on existential terms.

Beyond words, they shape our life,
in how we live and experience life.

Choose to speak and act for the larger good,
Peace will follow, as truth is understood.

··· ✶ ···

ENDINGS & NEW BEGINNINGS

···In every goodbye, a new promise awaits – are you ready?···

Goodbye, a word both heavy and light,
A trace of longing and a promise in sight,
It carries the sight of a road now gone,
With signs of roads where life moves on.

A chapter ends, its story complete,
An end that heralds a new chapter to greet.
The bitter tears of a parting embrace,
Are comforted by the hope of a new embrace.

In memories, we carry what will never go,

The smile that stays, wherever we go.
Goodbye is a lesson, though painful to learn,
It reminds us that some chapters must turn.

From endings, spring new hopes to explore,
A new chapter, ready for what's in store.
Life is a journey of goodbyes and hellos,
A pulse that endlessly comes and goes.

As we part, let's not despair,
For goodbye is also a promise we share.
And though the horizon may seem far,
We carry each other wherever we are.

FRIENDSHIP

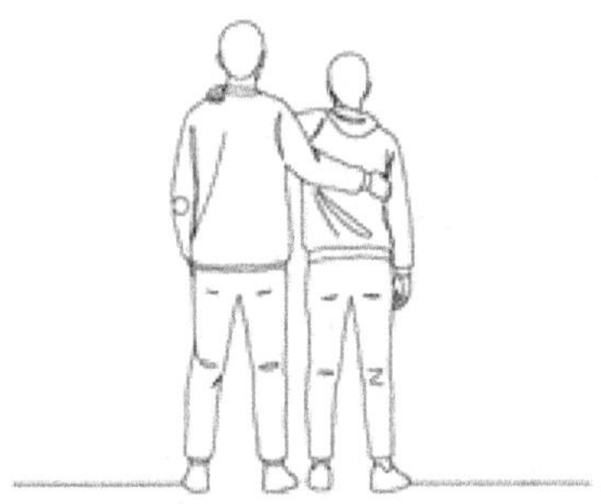

True friends don't always wear a smile,
Like a storm clearing the skies,
Their truths may sting, but they bring light,
Guiding us back to what is right.

Real friends speak with honest care,
Like a compass pointing ahead,
Their words may pinch, but they're sincere,
Showing the way, far and near.
Brave friends rise strong when doubt is near,

Like a mountain that never disappears,
They stand their ground through storm and rain,
Speaking wisdom, easing our pain.

Faithful friends love without conditions,
Like the sun shining, ever bright,
They give their care with hearts so pure,
A bond that stands the test of time.

Kind friends embrace us as we are,
Like the night embracing every star,
Through every flaw, they see your worth,
A constant presence grounding your earth.

Loyal friends value trust and loyalty,
Like roots that hold a sturdy tree,
They anchor us through highs and lows,
A strength that deepens endlessly.

Friendship is an overlap of lives.
A connection that transcends time,
A gift of love, pure and kind.

⋯ ✳ ⋯

BAD FRIENDSHIP

Beneath the smiles, it's deceit and lie,
And with the truth, it starts to die.

A smile that hides a secret scheme,
Words are sweet, not what they seem.

In friendship's cloak, they play their game
A trust betrayed, a heart in flame.

A hand extended, masked in grace,
Lies, Lust or Greed behind the face.

A friend who turns when shadows fall,
Was never really there at all.

TWO SOULS

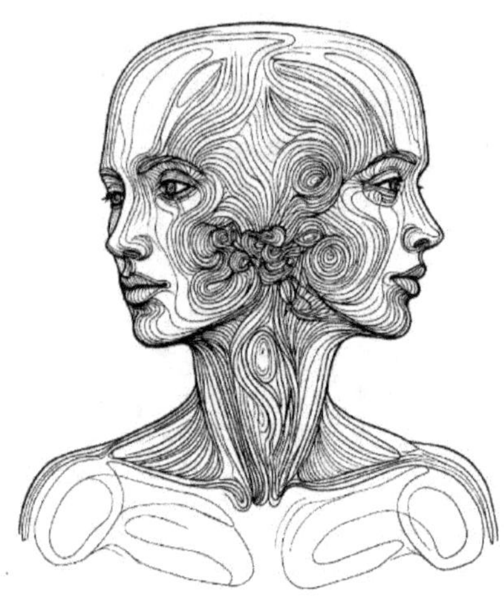

One which laments for the ignorant mind,
One which delights for the wise and kind.

One which laments for the path so tangled,
One which delights for the simple, yet angled.

One which laments for the chances missed,
One which delights in the efforts to persist.

One which laments for the 'close yet far',
One which delights for the 'just in par'.

One which laments for hopes betrayed,
One which delights for the help that stayed.

One which laments for the deer that fell,
One which delights in the tiger's yell.

One which laments for the fallen and low,
One which delights for the triumphs that glow.

For within me resides not one, but two,
Two souls that dance, in shades anew.

THE INNER DIALOGUE

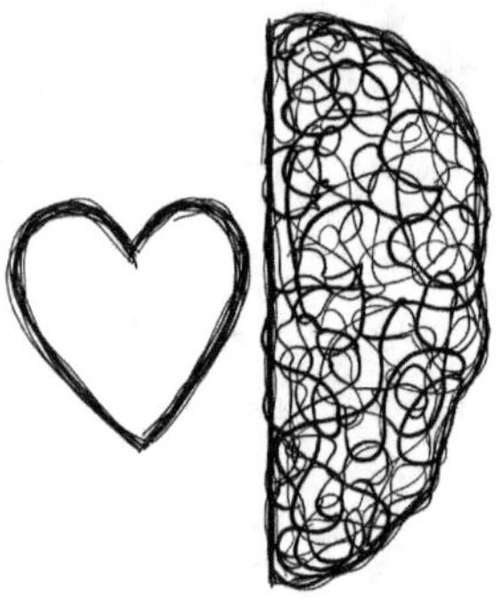

The Heart & Mind may disagree,
One reveals dreams, another reality.
Heart says, 'Fly! Go chase the Sun',
Mind informs softly, 'The risks aren't done'.

Heart's a breeze, quick to steer,
Mind's the river, deep and sincere.
Heart and Mind, might seem apart,
One Logical, another an Art.

Listen to the Heart, feel the beat,

In its rhythm, find joy and greet.

Trust the mind for a steady guide,

Remain safe, before the tide goes high.

Emotion, the juicier part of thought.
Thought, the guiding part of emotion.
The way one Thinks, is the way one Feels!

Together they dance, both creative and true,

Look at them both and find what's you.

··· ✸ ···

WEIGHT OF THE PAST

The past is a memory, a distant trace,
A moment gone, time and place.
Yet we hold it close, bound and tied,
Carry its weight deep inside.

Past is for reference, not to remain,
Where lessons linger, showing the way.
But dwelling there, we miss the gift,
Gift of Now, the living moment.

Look at the past with eyes that learn,
Acceptance of Past is freedom in turn.
The past has shaped, but not defined,
The truth of One's Heart and Mind.

Release the Weight of Past,
Live the now, The only time there is,
For life unfolds in the here and now,
The present moment is where Joy is.

GOOD OR BAD

···Who defines what's right or wrong?
Us or life itself? Read on...···

Life makes no judgement call,
No mark of good or bad at all.

It simply is and doesn't bind,
No rules of right or wrong, we'll find.

It's only Humans, hearts and minds,
Who measure worth in ways confined.

In social webs, they cast their views,
To sort the many shades and hues.

Life stands, both calm and clear,

No praise to seek, no blame to fear.

Do the Right, and Right shall flow,
Do the Wrong, and the wrong will flow.

Fairness lies in simple grace,

Results reflect the steps we traced.

No lines of good or bad are drawn,

In sensible living, we are reborn.

··· ✳ ···

WEALTH AND WELLBEING

Wealth makes the outside shine,

A tool we crafted, not divine.

Wellbeing, though, is the inner art,

A peaceful soul and a joyful heart.

Wealth is a means, not the final goal,

A piece of the puzzle, not the whole.
A pleasant life needs more than gold,
True joy is within, an integrity to hold.

A means, not an end, this wealth we make,
But to worship it fully is a grave mistake.
If wealth fills the pocket, it serves us right,
But in the head, it fuels a plight.

Pleasantness takes many forms,
In body, health and wealth bestow,
In mind, it's peace and love that grow,
When both align, we truly see,
Well-being is life's truest key.

Success isn't wealth alone,
It's overall joy, in harmony.
Outer riches and inner peace,
Together, bring life's true bliss.

... ✳ ...

THE MANY SHADES OF RELATIONSHIPS

...Which relationship in your life has shaped you the most – how did it change you?...

In the garden of souls, where relationships take root,

Each bond is a flower, tender and absolute.

Husband and wife, like oars in a stream,
Together they row, building their dream.

Parents and children, like roots and the tree,
Stability and growth, as strong as can be.

Siblings, like the sun and moon so bright,
Different, yet shining in shared light.

Teacher and student, like a lamp's steady glow,
Spreading knowledge, helping minds grow.

Grandparents and kids, like a treasure and key,
Unlocking wisdom with love's guarantee.

Friends, like mirrors reflecting our cheer,
Standing by us, year after year.

Colleagues, like gears in a well-built clock,
Working in harmony, steady and strong.

Neighbours, like fences and gardens in bloom,
Close, yet respecting each other's room.

Strangers, like stars in the vast, endless sky,
Unseen, but part of a world where we lie.

Beyond the bond, a deeper truth we find,
When souls align and spirits are combined.

THE THORN AND THE ROSE

The thorn spoke with a bitter tone,
'Why must I guard you all alone?
With edges sharp, I bear the pain,
Yet only your beauty earns the gain'.

The rose replied with a gentle grace,
'Oh thorn, my shield in this perilous place,
Without your strength, I'd surely fade,
Your watchful care keeps me unafraid'.

'They curse my name', the thorn did sigh,

'They call me cruel; they question why.
They love your bloom, your velvet hue,
But scorn my presence, harsh and true'.

'Do not despair', the rose then said,
'For without you, I'd hang my head.
Your strength unseen is my delight,
You hold me steady; you are my strength'.

'If I am strength', the thorn replied,
'Then you are beauty, nature's pride.
Together we stand, a perfect pair,
A bond of love, beyond compare'.

'And so', said the rose, 'let them adore,
For in my bloom, there's something more.
A silent truth that no one knows,
Your courage blooms in every rose'.

THE LOTUS AND HUMAN LIFE

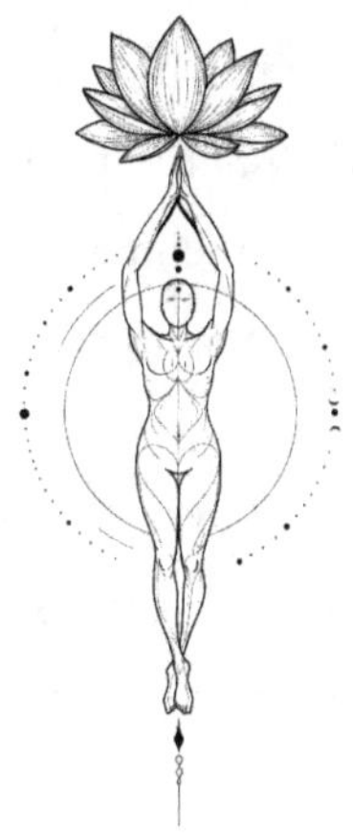

In murky waters, the lotus grows,
Untouched by the filth that life bestows.

It mirrors our spirit, steadfast and strong,
Teaching us the courage to journey along.

Untouched by dirt, the lotus stays pure,

A symbol of grace, calm and secure.
Amidst the mess, we rise and grow,
Purifying our minds as we go.

Its roots stay grounded, deep and strong,
Nurtured by earth, where they belong.
Through trials, we remember who we are,
Holding onto our roots, no matter how far.

With petals that turn toward the sun,
The lotus awakens as the day begun.
Like the lotus, we rise with might,
Embracing positivity in life's light.

Through seasons of drought, it survives,
Finding ways to keep hope alive.
Like the lotus, we persevere,
Facing challenges without fear.

The lotus, serene in its way,
Teaches us to live day by day.

In every challenge, we find a way,
Rising above, come what may.

NAVARATRI

···Navaratri: Where devotion meets divine celebration.···

Nine nights of joy, devotion and light,
Navaratri shines so pure and bright.

Each day a prayer, each night a song,
To the Goddess, our hearts belong.

In vibrant colours, we dance and praise,
Her power guiding all our ways.

From darkness to light, we seek her grace,
In every moment, in every place.

Durga, Lakshmi, Saraswati divine,
Through these nights, their blessings align.

Strength, wealth, wisdom they bestow,
In Navaratri's sacred glow.

DIWALI

···Word by word celebration of diwali···

Radiate, appreciate, create.

Ignite, delight, decorate.

Inspire, rejoice, captivate.

Celebrate, illuminate and elevate.

Rejuvenate, unite, motivate.

Spread love, embrace, resonate.

Shine bright, uplift, dedicate.

Together, we dream and celebrate.

Cherish, flourish, participate.

Share joy, bring hope, cultivate.

Give thanks, bring peace and liberate.

With hearts aglow, let's celebrate.
'Happy Diwali'!

··· ✳ ···

CHESS: THE KING'S GAMBIT

···In life's Chess, are you winning?···

Upon the board, in black and white,
A battle is born, of mind & not might.
Silent warriors, standing side by side,
Strategy and tactics, their only guide.

Knights leap forth, bishops glide,
Rooks stand firm, with patient pride.
Pawns advance with courage strong,
Queen commands and races along.

In chess, the game of life unfolds,
With wisdom guiding, what it holds.
Some battles won, some lessons learned,
In every turn, our fate is earned.

Guard your heart, defend your dream,
The board is vast, though small it seems.
And with each move, both bold and wise,
We live, We learn and We rise.

STOCK MARKET

···Can you predict the breakout, or will you wait for the crash?···

In a world of numbers, fast and vast,
The stock market moves with rhythm fast.
Up and down, the prices move,
As traders watch with eyes keen.

Support holds strong when prices fall,
Resistance stands, a barrier tall.
The trend line guides through every shift,
A charted way, through every shift.

Candlesticks print, green and red,
Telling tales of what happened.
A multi-bagger waits unsaid,
With hope of wealth ahead.

Bulls and bears in a tug of war,
Each battling to shift the market's score.
A breakout calls when the pressure's high,
But beware – a crash may come nearby.

Futures and options fuel the game,
The risk is sharp; the chances play.
The market swings, with highs and lows,
Where fortunes grow and danger shows.

Patience and strategy pave the way,
To make the most of each new day.
Trade with knowledge, Invest with care,
In every move, the stakes are there.

⁜

WARRIORS OF EMERGENCY OPERATIONS

···As we read this poem, somewhere across the world, people are involved in emergency operations. A dedication to them.···

When shadow grows long and emergency takes hold,
In the heartbeat of chaos, they rise fierce and bold.

Sirens awake, slicing through the haze,
As the frontline readies for the coming maze.

No margin for error, no room for delay,
In the heart of the chaos, they live the way.

Hands with purpose, Mind with fire,
Every second decides, and the stakes rise higher.

Each second a puzzle, each choice a thin line,
Between safety and ruin, they wrestle with time.

In the midst of the storm's roar,
They stand at the edge, defending the shore.

For the unsung heroes of the crisis unseen,
Bravery shines through the flickering screen.

WISDOM FROM THE ELEMENTS

···See how beautifully the Elements guide us.···

'Hold the storm in your hands', said the Sea
'It is not here to break you, but to shape you'.

'Walk through the flame', urged the Fire.
'You will emerge, not as ash, but as gold'.

'Trust the silence', murmured the Wind.
'For it holds the answers that noise cannot give'.

'Embrace the cracks in your heart', said the Mountain
'Through them, love finds its way in'.

'Fear not the fall', whispered the Sky
'Because that, too, is part of the flight'.

'For every challenge is a teacher', said Life with grace,
'And through each trial, you find your place'.

··· ✳ ···

FREEDOM & RESPONSIBILITY

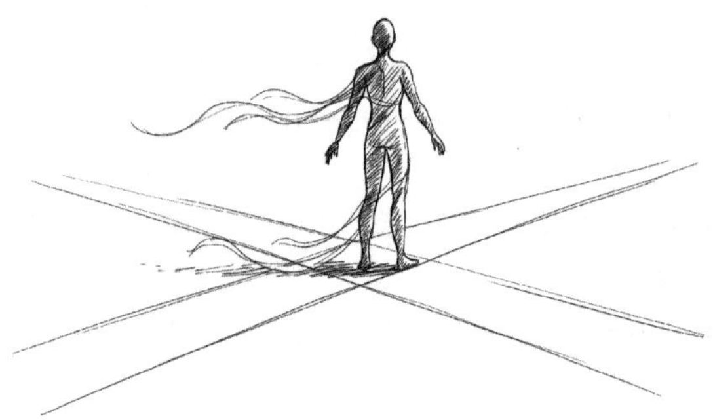

Freedom walks with responsibility's hand,
Together, they shape the life we've planned.

To live unbound, yet wisely true,
Our choices build the world anew.

With freedom's gift comes duty's call,
To rise, to care and to stand for all.

For what we choose affects the rest,

In shared respect, we do our best.

Freedom thrives where wisdom leads,
Responsibility guides through noble deeds.

… ✳ …

PURPOSE OF LIFE?

···When was the last time you stopped searching and just enjoyed being alive?···

Elementary minds will always seek,
A purpose for life, a goal unique.
But if life's meaning were destined,
Life's flowering would be concealed.

This question grows when life feels small,
Unworthy, mundane, lacking it all.
In joy and bliss, such questions will fall,
With no need to question life at all.

We are life itself, pure and whole.
Relationships, business are treasures we hold,
What we are and what we have,
Are two separate truths, not parallel or the
same.

When the circus of thought grows larger than
life,
This question arises, bringing an inner strife.
Life is boundless, with no purpose to chase,
That's what makes it a boundless space.

⋯ ✶ ⋯

THE CONQUEST OF TIME

···Are you chasing time, or is time chasing you?···

Living life is a blend of time and energy,
A transient journey all beings must take.
Time on this planet is tied in tune,
To the sun, the stars and the shining moon.

Time is a dimension of life,
Not a concept, nor a thought.
Whether one acts or lets it be,
It flows on, endlessly free.

In time, things begin, they grow and they end,
Change is a force that none can suspend.
In time, lives find their place to be,
Mastering time shapes destiny.

Time feels relative to the human mind,
In joy, it races, leaving moments behind.
In sorrow, it lingers, dragging so slow,
Shifting pace in its endless flow.

With sharp perception and intelligence
profound,
Manage self-qualities with wisdom abound.
Align with the rhythm of Time's steady chime,
Adapt, perceive and stay ahead of time.
Conquering oneself is the conquest of time.

THE MYTH OF PERFECTION

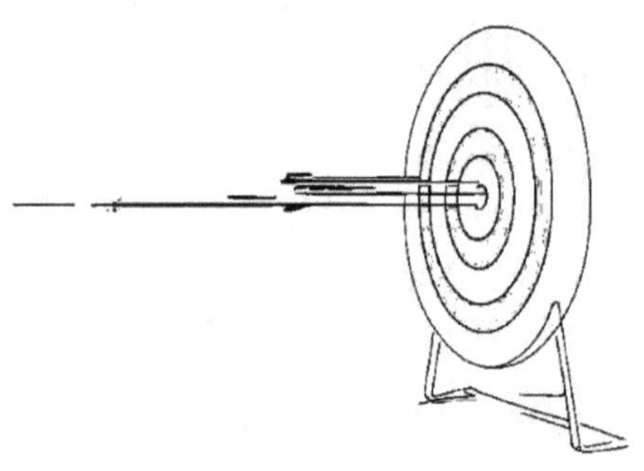

···Do you find peace in progress, or is perfection still your pursuit?···

All of life is a journey,

From partial to perfection.

A path we repeat,

Perfection is a mirage, elusive indeed.

What seems perfect,

Will evolve or transform.

Perfection is an elusive aim,

Progress is real, the steady force.

To chase perfection is a weary race,
Fatigue and anger take their place.
Disappointment lingers in the chase,
When perfection keeps us in its race.

In pursuit of perfection, the path is clear,
Progress and consistency are all we need here.
Embrace the journey, mistakes and all,
For each correction helps us stand tall.

THE SACRED SILENCE

···Is silence your sanctuary or your fear?···

Silence is

Pause – the space between thoughts, where wisdom arises

Stillness – the stillness of the soul, where truth speaks

Quiet – the absence of noise, the presence of the divine

Calm – the surrender of the mind, the peace of the heart

Tranquillity – the harmony of being, untouched
by the world
Serenity – the acceptance of what is, free from
resistance
Peace – the quiet within, where the soul is at
home
Rest – the letting go, the renewal of the spirit
Reflection – the mirror of the mind, where
self-discovery begins
Solitude – the sacred space of inner connection
Repose – the stillness of the body and soul in
unity

Silence is a source of great strength.

THE DOUBLE EDGE OF SECRETS

···Some secrets heal, others hurt... Ready to discover why?···

A secret can be **Wisdom**,

A quiet knowing where strength begins.

A secret can also be **Deception**,

The lies one tells to hide the fears.

A secret can be **Trust**,

The bond one builds, a promise unbroken.

A secret can also be **Partition**,

The distance it creates between soul and kin.

A secret can be a **Mystery**,

A mask that sparks curiosity and wonder.

A secret can also be **Betrayal**,

The trust, it shatters in a bond once cherished.

A secret can be **Strength**,

The silent courage to bear what others don't
know.

A secret can also be **Guilt**,

The weight it places in the keeper's heart.

A secret can be **Hope**,

The potential dream, where possibility grows.

A secret can be **Fear**,

The constant unease of exposure's sting.

A secret's worth lies in its Intent,

It can shield or shatter, build or torment.

Its power lies not in what is concealed,
But in the truth it seeks to reveal.

··· ✳ ···

NO MATTER WHAT

Through storm and calm, the rivers flow,
The sun may rise, the moon may glow,
The tides may shift, the winds may gust,
We maintain Integrity, no matter what.

In love's embrace or when it fades,
When dreams dissolve or hopes cascade,
Through joy, through grief, through endless
strut,
We hold on to our strength, no matter what.

The mountain's high, the valley deep,

The promises we strive to keep,

In loss, in gain, through doubt or trust,

We move forward, no matter what.

Though days are short and nights are long,

The heart grows weak, but souls stay strong,

Through all life brings, shade or sun,

We rise again – no matter what.

For in each trial, a spark is lit,

We find our strength, no matter what.

··· ✳ ···

VICTORY

*···Is victory about winning, or the
journey that shapes you?···*

Victory isn't just the final score,
It's the heart that keeps striving for more.

Victory is born from the fire within,
A journey of strength, where dreams begin.

It's the sweat and the tears, the lessons they
bring,
The patience to wait while your spirit takes
wing.

It's the battles you fight in the depths of your
soul,
Turning each setback into a step toward your
goal.

*It's the courage to rise when you stumble and
fall,*
To stand even stronger, to answer the call.

Victory is not just the cheers or the fame,
It's finding your purpose, igniting the flame.

For true victory lives in the heart of the brave,
In the love for the journey, not what you crave.

So march with resolve, let your spirit soar,
Victory is yours when you strive for more.

THE JOURNEY BEYOND

···Is Death the greatest mystery – what's your perspective?···

Death is a door to the unknown shore,
A silent passage, we fear but explore.
In silence, it waits with gentle grace,
Guiding each soul to its resting place...

It holds no malice, bears no hate,
A timeless keeper of every fate.
Neither wealth nor power can delay,
For all must walk its quiet way.

This body, a loan from Earth's embrace,

To honour and use with mindful grace.

With care, we build; with love, repay,

And return it whole at the end of our stay.

Born we are, with death to face,

A truth that guides through time and space.

This mortal fate, a force so clear,

Awakens souls to seek what's near.

As *life is, so is death,*
In *living fully, we find our breath.*
Only those who embrace the end,

Can live completely, their souls transcend.

It marks not the end but a path anew,

A bridge to worlds beyond our view.

In its stillness, all sorrows cease,

A final breath, a quiet peace.

THE CONTROL OF TONGUE

···What would change if you spoke only with love, even in the most heated moments?···

Speak less, listen more, let thoughts be clear,
In stillness, the soul finds calm and cheer.
True strength lies in knowing when to remain quiet,
And when to speak, letting words ignite.

A calm tongue keeps the heart serene,
Keeper of tranquillity, pure and clean.
Control over speech is control over self,
A treasure greater than any worldly wealth.

Tame the tongue and tame the storm,
In talking sensible, we'll find the heart's true
form.
Tongue has the power to make or break,
So speak with love, for harmony's sake.

In every moment, let wisdom reign,
For spoken words can ease or bring pain.
Choose your speech with thoughtful grace,
And let peace reflect on your face.

THE POWER OF PATIENCE

···What if patience is the secret ingredient to everything you've been waiting for?···

Patience is the silent strength we hold,
A force more precious than silver or gold.
It builds resilience, steady and true,
Turning storms into skies of blue.

With time as its ally, dreams ascend,
Through patient toil until the journey's end.
Like rivers carving valleys, slow and sure,
Success comes to those who can endure.

In chaos, where storms often grow,
Patience keeps its calm like a peaceful undertow.
In relationships, patience gently sows,
Seeds of empathy, where hearts can grow.

To pause, reflect and let wisdom steer,
Patience transforms haste into a vision clear.
In quiet soil, a seed must wait.
Patience teaches that all things are worth the
wait.

Each hardship endured with patience,
Strengthens the heart, makes it whole.

In time, patience reveals its worth,
Guiding through each trial on Earth.
For those who trust its gentle might,
Life unfolds, brilliant and bright.

··· ✳ ···

STRENGTH IN FORGIVENESS

···If you could forgive yourself for one thing today, what would it be?···

Forgiveness, a quiet balm for the soul,

Healing the wounds that time cannot control.

To forgive is not forgetting the past,

But acceptance of the change in heart.

Healing both forgiver and forgiven,

Creating space for peace to be given.

Inner peace grows where forgiveness reigns,

Unchaining the heart, dissolving its pains.

Transforming pain into something new,
With growth & understanding in all that we do.
True strength is found in moving ahead,
Past the hurts, to peace instead.

*Empathy and compassion look beyond the
wrong,
Accepting the struggle, where hearts grow
strong.*

True power in life is found within,
In the courage to forgive and begin,
Breaking the cycle, we rise above,
With open hearts and endless love.

JOURNEY OF SELF-DISCOVERY

…If your journey of self-discovery were a book, what chapter are you in right now?…

The journey of self-discovery begins,

When one remains true to oneself,

When one gives all of their heart,

And soul into endeavours.

When 'I don't know' takes its place,

Opening the mind to life's vast space.

It ventures through, known & unknown,
Re-evaluating beliefs, seeking new truths,
Exploring the depths of what's yet unseen,
Listening deeply to what lies between.

Carrying a mind unsullied and clear,
Not bound by the past, nor driven by fear.
With perception clear, one remains true,
On the steadfast path of self to pursue.

Living sensibly, Honouring humanity,
Striving for the larger well-being,
These values direct, both steady and sure,
Guiding the journey toward a self that's pure.

THE RESILIENCE OF THE HUMAN SPIRIT

···What lesson has a setback taught you about your own strength?···

The human spirit, not defined by fall,
But by the strength to rise through it all.
Like a phoenix that rises from the ashes,
It soars again, undaunted.

In a quiet struggle, it finds its voice,
Turning pain into power, making choices.
Like a seed pushing through the dirt,
Growing towards the light.

Like steel that's forged in fire's embrace,

It bends and bends, but never breaks.

Through every trial, it learns to soar,

A quiet strength at its core.

Like the tide that pulls back only to rise higher,

Always finding its way forward.

Not without fear, but with the courage to move,
The spirit persists, with strength to prove.
Like a mountain climber, facing peak,

Keeps climbing, no matter how steep.

Through every trial, the spirit grows strong,

Resilience is the fire that keeps us moving on.

··· ✳ ···

HUMAN IMAGINATION

···What story does your imagination want to tell the world? Start writing it now.···

Human imagination is a limitless engine of possibility,
Like a river carving a path through mountains with agility.
It flows unbound, creating ways,
Transforming dreams into reality's gaze.

Human imagination is the bridge between dreams and reality,

Like a rainbow uniting two lands of serenity.
It spans the gap, both vast and wide,
Where fantasy and logic walk side by side.

Human imagination is the light that guides
innovation,
Like a lighthouse leading through the fog of
convention.
It pierces the custom, shows a new way,
Inspiring minds to seize the day.

Human imagination is the spark that fuels
creativity,
Like the dawn that breaks the night's captivity.
It begins with a thought, then expands the mind,
Transforming the ordinary into something
refined.

*Human imagination is the voice of a world yet
to come,*
Like a melody hummed before the drum.
It stirs the mind, then sets its course,
A vision shaping the future's course.

··· ✳ ···

KARMA AND FREEWILL

···Are we prisoners of the past, or architects of the now?···

The past remains with its traces intact,
A mark of thoughts, emotions and act.
Karma follows as life proceeds,
A natural law of actions and deeds.

Karma is not reward or blame,
It's cause and effect and works the same.
What we touched, in thought or deed,
Lingers as a part of what we did.

The present moment is ours to steer,
A chance to act with purpose clear.
Though the past may echo, its weight will fade,
If we choose consciously, new paths are laid.

Yesterday's actions cannot be undone,
But today's choices have just begun.
Free will or bondage lies in the now,
It is in our hands what we allow.

Memory persists; it guides and informs,
But it is in this moment that life transforms.
Regret or learning, the choice is ours,
The future depends on how we restore.

Handle the present with conscious care,
And shape our lives with actions fair.
Karma follows, but free will is always ours,
Every moment shapes our destiny's door.

… ✳ …

THE ROAD WE CHOOSE

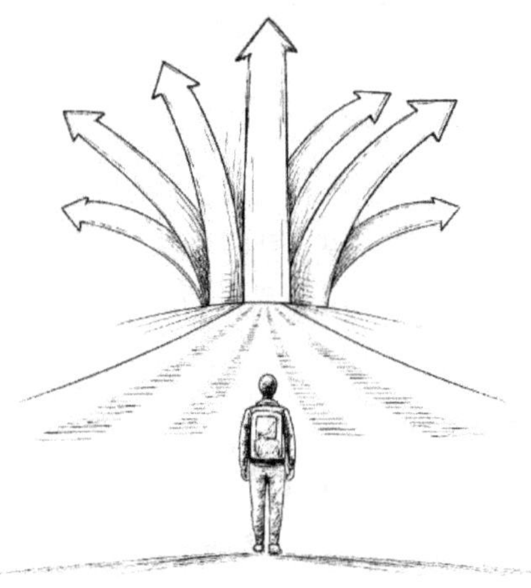

People do not decide their future;

They decide their habits,

And their habits decide their future.

People do not decide their future;

They decide their choices,

And their choices decide their destinies.

People do not decide their future;

They decide their actions,

And their actions shape their tomorrows.

People do not decide their future;

They decide their attitudes,

And their attitudes decide their outcomes.

People do not decide their future;

They decide their values,

And their values guide their journey.

People do not decide their future;

They decide their priorities,

And their priorities set their course.

People do not decide their future;

They decide their reactions,

And their reactions shape their fate.

People do not decide their future;

They decide their perspectives,

And their perspectives colour their world.

So, while the future remains unknown, its seeds
lie within,
In the choices we make and the journeys we
pin.

... ✳ ...

QUESTIONS & ANSWERS

1. What is Good?

Good indeed is living a life of virtue

Even greater is living without causing harm to others.

Greater still is cultivating wisdom and compassion within oneself.

Greatest of all is using that wisdom and compassion to uplift others.

In doing so, one embodies the highest form of goodness.

2. What is Bad?

Bad indeed is the life wasted in ignorance.

Even worse is harming others for selfish gains.

Worse still is nurturing hatred and greed within.

Worst of all is forgetting the purpose of existence.

If one indulges in these, Suffering is bound to continue endlessly.

3. What is Truth?

Truth indeed is knowing oneself as part of the universe.

Even rarer is the ability to see beyond illusions.

Even rarer still is living by truth despite challenges.

Rarest of all is the courage to uphold truth for other's welfare.

If one does so, worldly suffering is transcended.

4. What is Happiness?

Happiness indeed is the absence of desires.

Even greater is finding joy in simple moments.

Even greater still is bringing joy to others selflessly.

Greatest of all is the bliss of a mind in harmony.

If one achieves this, ultimate peace is attained.

5. What is Success?

Success indeed is fulfilling one's duty with sincerity.

Even greater is succeeding without harming others.

Greater still is achieving success while uplifting others.

Greatest of all is inner fulfilment, free of ego or greed.

If one finds this, Life is fruitful.

6. What is Wisdom?

Wisdom indeed is understanding the impermanence of life.

Even rarer is the ability to discern right from wrong.

Rarer still is applying wisdom in daily actions.

Rarest of all is sharing wisdom to guide others.

If one does so, the path to liberation is open.

7. What is Strength?

Strength indeed is enduring life's hardships with grace.

Even greater is standing for what is just and true.

Greater still is conquering one's own fears and desires.

Greatest of all is the strength that uplifts and protects others.

If one embodies this, one becomes truly invincible.

8. What is Time?

Time indeed is the constant flow of existence.
Even more precious is the moment lived with awareness.
More precious still is time used for selfless deeds.
Most precious of all is time spent in pursuit of wisdom.
If one values time, one will be Victorious.

9. What is Death?

Death indeed is the inevitable end of the body.
Even deeper is understanding it as part of life's cycle.
Deeper still is accepting it without fear or regret.
Deepest of all is realising that Life transcends death.
If one knows this, he/she lives and dies in peace.

10. What is Love?

Love indeed is caring for another without
expectation.
Even greater is love that sees no boundaries or
differences.
Greater still is love that forgives and heals
wounds.
Greatest of all is universal love that unites all
beings.
If one embodies this, one becomes a source of
divinity.

11. What is Freedom?

Freedom indeed is being free from external
chains.
Even greater is freedom from mental and
emotional bondage.
Greater still is the freedom that comes from
self-realisation.
Greatest of all is liberation from the cycle of
birth and death.
If one attains this, one is truly free.

12. What is Wealth?

Wealth indeed is having enough to meet one's needs.

Even greater is the wealth of health and knowledge.

Greater still is the wealth of virtuous relationships.

Greatest of all is the wealth of inner contentment.

One who finds this, becomes the richest of all.

13. What is Peace?

Peace indeed is a life free of conflict and strife.

Even deeper is peace within one's own heart.

Deeper still is spreading peace to others through kindness.

Deepest of all is the peace of union with the infinite.

If one achieves this, true liberation is attained.

14. What is Failure?

Failure indeed is not achieving what was desired.

Even worse is failing to learn from one's mistakes.

Worse still is giving up and losing faith in oneself.

Worst of all is failing to live a virtuous and meaningful life.

If one overcomes this, failure is transformed into wisdom.

15. What is Forgiveness?

Forgiveness indeed is letting go of anger and resentment.

Even greater is forgiving without expecting an apology.

Greater still is forgiving oneself for past mistakes.

Greatest of all is forgiving with compassion and understanding.

If one does this, Inner freedom and peace are achieved.

16. What is Courage?

Courage indeed is facing fear and uncertainty.

Even greater is standing up for truth despite opposition.

Greater still is persevering through life's hardest trials.

Greatest of all is the courage to walk the spiritual path.

If one does so, greatness is achieved in life.

17. What is Humility?

Humility indeed is knowing one's limits.

Even greater is serving others without seeking praise.

Greater still is acknowledging the divinity in others.

Greatest of all is humility before the infinite truth.

If one embodies this, the highest wisdom is attained.

18. What is Justice?

Justice indeed is treating others fairly and equally.

Even deeper is standing up for the oppressed.

Deeper still is acting without bias or selfish gain.

Deepest of all is justice guided by compassion and truth.

If one pursues this, one becomes a beacon of righteousness.

19. What is Destiny?

Destiny indeed is the result of past actions and choices.

Even deeper is understanding its interplay with free will.

Deeper still is shaping destiny through righteous action.

Deepest of all is transcending destiny through self-realisation.

If one achieves this, one becomes the master of his/her fate.

20. What is a Friend?

A friend indeed is someone who supports and cares.

Even greater is a friend who speaks truth when needed.

Greater still is a friend who uplifts you spiritually.

Greatest of all is the friend who reflects the
divine in you.
If one finds such a friend, one is truly blessed.

21. What is a Meaningful Life?
A meaningful life indeed is one filled with
virtue.
Even greater is living in service to others and the
world.
Greater still is a life spent in the pursuit of truth.
Greatest of all is a life that leads to
self-realisation.
If one achieves this, the highest purpose of
existence is fulfilled.